Ida and Jake's Game Night

by Katy Wischow • illustrated by Elisa Rocchi

Lucy Calkins and Michael Rae-Grant, Series Editors

LETTER-SOUND CORRESPONDENCES

all consonants, all short vowels, ff, ll, ss, zz, ck, ch, sh, th, wh, ng, CV words

n(k), tch, a(l, ll), a_e, i_e, o_e, u_e, e_e, -es, -ing, -ed, o(ld, st), -y = /ē/, ea, ee, ai, ay, oa, ow = /ō/, igh, oo, -le, ar, or, er

HIGH-FREQUENCY WORDS

as, do, his, is, says, the, to, was, you

your, what, want, have, done, here, love, said, don't, won't, any, always, goes, know, one, **could**

Ida and Jake's Game Night
Author: Katy Wischow
Series Editors: Lucy Calkins and Michael Rae-Grant

Heinemann
145 Maplewood Avenue, Suite 300
Portsmouth, NH 03801
www.heinemann.com

Copyright © 2023 Heinemann and The Reading and Writing Project Network, LLC

All rights reserved, including but not limited to the right to reproduce this book, or portions thereof, in any form or by any means whatsoever, without written permission from the publisher. For information on permission for reproductions or subsidiary rights licensing, please contact Heinemann at permissions@heinemann.com. Heinemann's authors have devoted their entire careers to developing the unique content in their works, and their written expression is protected by copyright law. We respectfully ask that you do not adapt, reuse, or copy anything on third-party (whether for-profit or not-for-profit) lesson-sharing websites.
—Heinemann Publishers

"Dedicated to Teachers" is a trademark of Greenwood Publishing Group, LLC.

Cataloging-in-Publication data is on file with the Library of Congress.

ISBN-13: 978-0-325-13902-9

Design and Production: Dinardo Design LLC, Carole Berg, and Rebecca Anderson

Editors: Anna Cockerille and Jennifer McKenna

Illustrations: Elisa Rocchi

Photographs: p. 32 (Senet game) © Federica Milella/Shutterstock; p. 32 (Go game) © Bragin Alexey/Shutterstock.

Manufacturing: Gerard Clancy

Printed in the United States of America on acid-free paper
3 4 5 6 7 8 9 10 MP 28 27 26 25 24 23
January 2023 printing / PO# 4500866759

Contents

1 Game Night 1

2 Yank! 11

3 The Puzzle 23

Game Night

"Jake's here!" calls Ida
as she lets her pal in.
"We can start!"

"I love game night!" Jake says.

"We ALL do!" Ida adds.

Ida picks a game to start. "This game is the coolest," she tells Jake. "You win if you drive your car the fastest."

Ida drives her car along the board.

"Nine...ten. Almost at the finish line! I'm going to win!" she cheers.

"Not if I catch up!" teases Mama.

"*Vroom vroom!* I'm coming for you!"

"Nooooo!" Ida giggles.

Jake's car is right after Mama's.

"I'm coming too!" he calls.

Mom smiles. "Looks like I'm the slowest."

"That's okay, Mom!" Ida says.

After Ida wins, she stands up and waves her arms.

"I'm the champ! I'm the champ! Number one!" she cheers.

Jake groans. "We *know*, Ida.

We get it. You won. You *always* win!"

Mama says, "Ida, what have we said? It's fun to win. But you have to be a good sport too."

"Jake gets to pick

the next game," says Mom.

"I pick...my puzzle!" Jake says.

Ida scrunches up her nose.

"Noooo, not a *puzzle!*

Puzzles take ten *years* to do."

"Ida, you chose last time," says Mama.

"And you know Jake loves puzzles."

Ida sighs. "Okay...Let's try it."

2

Yank!

Jake adds a piece to the puzzle.

Mom adds a piece.

And Mama adds a piece.

Ida *wants to* add a piece, but…

"It won't fit!" she says.

She tries harder and harder.

She twists it this way and that way.

"Can I help?" asks Mama.

"No! I can do it!" says Ida.

She crosses her arms.

Ida catches Mom turning the piece. "Stop! I don't want any hints," she whines. "I can do it!"

"It's not that hard," says Jake. "Look, it goes right here!"

The puzzle gets bigger and bigger.

"We're almost done with it!" says Jake.

Ida holds up an odd-looking piece.

"That's a hard one!" says Mama.

"Let's ALL try it."

"No!" snaps Ida. "I can do it *myself!*"

Ida tries harder and harder. She twists the piece this way and that way.

Mama leans in and says, "You know, Ida, puzzles aren't something you can win. Let us help you."

Ida feels like a pot bubbling up.

She gets madder

and madder

and MADDER.

She HATES being no good at stuff!

She can't help it—
she YANKS the board, and
the whole puzzle falls apart.

"*Whoa,*" says Jake.

"That's it," says Mom.

"Game night is done."

3
The Puzzle

"Knock, knock," says Mom.

"Ida, that was not okay," says Mama.

"I know," Ida mumbles.

"What do you think it felt like for Jake when you flipped his puzzle?" asks Mama.

"I wish we could have played for longer," Ida mumbles.
"Me too," says Mom.

Ida hangs her head.

"I'm sorry!"

"We know," say Mom and Mama.

"What can you do to fix it?"

Ida thinks

    and thinks

        and THINKS.

Then, she grabs her markers,

and she starts to sketch and cut.

"Mom! Mama!
I came up with a way
to make things better!
Can I take this to Jake?"

> Learn about...

The History of Board Games

Senet

Board games have been around for thousands of years. One of the oldest board games we know of comes from Egypt, and it's called *Senet*. This beautiful Senet box is more than 3,000 years old.

Although most people have never heard of Senet, some very old board games are still popular today. *Chess* was invented more than 1,000 years ago—in India or China or Iran; historians are not quite sure. The oldest chess pieces discovered were carved from *ivory*—elephant tusks.

Go

A game called *Go* was invented about 2,500 years ago in China. Today, Go is still super popular in East Asia—so popular that there are television channels that just show Go games, the way we have channels that show basketball or baseball games here in the United States!

> Talk about...

Ask your reader some questions like...

- What happened in this book?
- Why did Ida yank the puzzle? What could she have done instead?

- In this book, Ida isn't a good sport. A *good sport* is someone who's fun to play with because they follow the rules, and they're nice to the other players. What are some ways to be a good sport?